D1014811

COPING
IN

A Blended
Family

Jane Hurwitz

FEB 2001
SALINAS PUBLIC LIBRARY

THE ROSEN PUBLISHING GROUP, INC./NEW YORK

Published in 1997 by The Rosen Publishing Group, Inc.
29 East 21st Street, New York, NY 10010

Copyright 1997 by Jane Hurwitz

All rights reserved. No part of this book may be reproduced in any form without permission in writing from the publisher, except by a reviewer.

First Edition

Library of Congress Cataloging-in-Publication Data

Hurwitz, Jane.
  Coping in a blended family / Jane Hurwitz.
    p. cm.
  Includes bibliographical references and index.
  Summary: Discusses the emotional and logistical challenges that can arise when two families become one through remarriage after a death or divorce.
  ISBN 0-8239-2077-1
  1. Stepfamilies—United States—Juvenile literature.
2. Stepparents—United States—Juvenile literature. 3. Children of divorced parents—United States—Juvenile literature.
[1. Stepfamilies.] I. Title.
HQ759.92.H88 1997
306.85—dc21   97-2470
                                                             CIP
                                                              AC

Manufactured in the United States of America

To my parents, Sue and Gene Hurwitz

ABOUT THE AUTHOR ◇

Jane Hurwitz earned an M.A. degree in economics from the University of Kansas. She has worked as a research assistant for the University of Nebraska and as a budget analyst for Yale University. She gained greater insight into some of the problems concerning failing family relationships while she was a board member at a battered women's shelter.

Jane is married and a parent. She is an avid gardener, and she loves to read.

The coauthor of *Sally Ride: Shooting for the Stars* and *Staying Healthy*, Jane is a full-time writer.

Contents

Introduction

What do President Bill Clinton, former President Ronald Reagan, actor Sylvester Stallone, and the television family the Brady Bunch all have in common? They all belong to stepfamilies.

The stepfamily, or blended family, is as common today as the traditional family headed by a biological mother and father. About 50 percent of all Americans currently have some sort of step relationship, from stepsibling to stepparent to stepgrandparent. There are many different types of families in the United States and around the world. For example, in a single-parent family, the children live with just one of their biological parents. That parent may find another adult to love, and ask him or her to move in and share the home. Unrelated people can form a family, as in adoption. The foster family and the communal family (related and unrelated people living together in one home) are also examples of families. Or, both parents can be of the same sex and adopt a child or have children from a previous marriage. As you can see, it takes more than biological connections to make a family.

Blended families are complicated. There are many different ways of becoming a blended family and many types of living arrangements. Blended families are normally formed through remarriage, often after divorce. The death of one parent can also lead to remarriage. A person with children may marry someone without kids, or both people may have children from past relationships (married or not). The children of one parent might visit only on the weekends, and are considered part of the blended family. If both parents are of the same sex, one or both may have children from previous heterosexual (opposite-sex) relationships. While gay and lesbian relationships are not recognized nationally as legal unions, they are still considered to be a blended family.

Whatever the circumstances, the blending of two different families in a step relationship is often difficult. Many new coparents expect their multihome stepfamily to be just like a traditional biological family. Blended families may try and avoid identifying themselves as such because of negative associations. But avoiding the differences can lead these families to have unrealistic expectations. And unrealistic expectations can lead to added stress and frustration. This book is about creating a blended family, how blended families are formed, and how people in the family are affected. The blended family is not the same as the traditional family, but that does not mean it is less meaningful or incapable of building strong emotional bonds. Blended families have to build shared memories and establish new ways of doing things. It takes time and effort to build good blended family relationships. But it can be done and it is done every day.

This book deals primarily with blended families that have formed by remarriage after death or divorce. But the problems and concerns of these blended families will translate easily into the confines of any type of blended family. Many experts are now challenging the common perception that the blended family is defined by marriage. One study suggests that about 50 percent of the 60 million children under the age of thirteen in this country are currently living with one biological parent and that parent's current partner—someone to whom the child is not biologically related. If your parents are gay or if your parents are not married, you potentially still have to deal with new emotional bonds, worry about divided loyalties, and integrate with new stepsiblings. While this book still maintains its focus around blended families formed by remarriage, it also addresses the problems and concerns of all types of blended families and provides you with practical solutions to common dilemmas. It will also help you adjust how you think about blended families and show the positive side of sharing your home with new family members.

One of the biggest issues facing blended families is the lack of available resources and absence of cultural rules and guidelines. Our cultural traditions focus primarily on intact, first-marriage families. Often the most ordinary events, from filling out a form to celebrating a holiday, can cause blended family members to feel uncomfortable and embarrassed. But there are organizations that are devoted entirely to blended family problems and solutions, offering therapy sessions, videos, pamphlets, and booklets for both parents and teens. These organizations recognize that applying methods and information specific to intact nuclear families can be destructive to the blended family.

Reading this book is the first step in helping your new family become a successful blended family. Recognizing your role in the family and how your feelings and actions contribute to your family's success is essential. When you are done reading, share this book with your new family. Together, you can help each other create realistic expectations and work towards living in a harmonious blended family.

CHAPTER 1

Blended Families: Not Just a Fairy Tale

Jill's Story

Shortly after the death of my mother, my father decided to remarry. I knew that no one could ever replace my mother, but my dad felt I needed a mother's influence and he needed the companionship of a wife.

My father soon found a woman who met his basic criteria and he quickly married her. My new stepmother was not accustomed to managing a home or money. Her two daughters were also lacking in this area.

While my dad worked long hours to support our new family, I was left alone in the house with people who were practically strangers. Without my dad's knowledge, I was forced to work like a servant in my own home. I cleaned, scrubbed, and cooked mountains of food for my stepfamily. I was constantly exhausted and miserable. My new stepsisters refused to share what previously had been my own room and I had to sleep in the basement among the ashes and cinders.

In this modern-day version of Cinderella, Jill didn't live in a traditional nuclear family. A nuclear family contains a husband, a wife, and children that those two parents have conceived or adopted. Jill's family can be considered one example of a "blended family."

What is a "blended family"? Is it fictional, like the story of Cinderella? Not at all. It may not mirror old myths like the story of Cinderella, but blended families are commonly found in everyday life. By calling a family "blended," we mean that the individuals in the family are linked by any combination of marriage, divorce (or death) and remarriage or cohabitation. Every blended family is unique, but they usually have two things in common:

- *Blended families include children.*
- *Blended families have at least one spouse who is a stepparent.*

These two sentences focus on the legal bonds of a blended family. Using the term stepparent implies the union of the parents is one of legal remarriage. However, sometimes a blended family is formed when two families join to share one household. The parents may not be married, but the family is still considered to be a blended one.

Using the term "blended" helps to describe the variations in different kinds of families. Blended means harmonious, and most families work to achieve harmony in their daily lives.

You cannot assume that a blended family will look or act like a conventional, nuclear family. But by expanding the definition of a family, you can understand that a blended family can be just as loving and harmonious as a traditional family.

Below are several examples of blended families:

Eric

Eric's father died when Eric was an infant. His mother remarried and had another child with Eric's stepfather. Eric's blended family has one parent, one stepparent, and one halfsibling.

Tonya

Tonya's parents divorced when she was five years old. She lives with her mother and new stepfather during the week. On weekends she lives with her father, stepmother, and two stepbrothers. Tonya's blended family includes two parents, two stepparents, and two stepsiblings.

Huynh

Huynh, her mother, and her two sisters fled Vietnam when Huynh was an infant. Her father was killed in the war in Vietnam soon after Huynh left. Once in the United States, Huynh and her family moved into her aunt's apartment. Huynh's mother later met a man who had also fled the war and resettled in America. They soon married. Huynh's blended family includes one parent, two sisters, and one stepparent.

Peter

Peter's mother divorced his father when Peter was two years old. She quickly remarried but divorced again only five years later. When Peter was ten, his mother married her third husband, who had two daughters from a previous marriage. Peter has had no contact with his biological father since he was two years old. Peter's blended family has one parent, two stepparents, and two stepsiblings.

MYTHS AND REALITIES

Even though the American family has changed drastically in the last fifty years, blended families are the type of family most often assumed to contain problems.

Fairy tales like Cinderella reflect common myths about blended families: evil stepmothers, cruel stepsiblings, and wholesome children like Cinderella in a family with no one to nurture them. These stereotypes have circulated for many generations, and they are still used unfairly. Before a blended family is created, however, families often experience major transitions. Stereotypes can add to the negative effects of these transitions. Experts believe there are at least sixty common myths that cause problems and intra-conflict in blended families. How a newly blended family handles conflicts caused by myths is crucial to the success of the family.

Rashad

Rashad and his three sisters lived in a small town of 2,000 people where news traveled fast. Everyone knew that Rashad's parents were getting a divorce. When summer arrived, Rashad was glad that he did not have to face his ninth-grade classmates for a while.

By the time school started in September, life was quite different for Rashad's family. His mother had moved with Rashad and his sisters to a small apartment in town near the grocery store. Rashad's father was living with his parents on their farm, about thirty miles from town.

In addition to his regular job as a mechanic, now Rashad's father also helped his parents on the farm in exchange for rent. He did not have much time to visit his children. Sometimes Rashad did not see his father for more than a week, but he did talk to him on the phone every night before bedtime.

Rashad missed his father, and he tried to understand that his parents were both working extra hard. He knew that maintaining separate living arrangements was much more expensive and time-consuming for his parents.

Rashad's younger sisters could not adjust to the new living arrangements. They constantly fought with each other while their mother was at work, and they complained when she was home. They were never happy, and they often refused to talk to their father on the phone.

While his mother worked, Rashad had to break up many fights between the girls. Even though he was not much older than his oldest sister, Rashad felt it necessary to assume many of his absent father's duties. He did not enjoy the responsibility, but someone needed to intervene between his sisters.

To make matters worse, when school started that fall, his parents could not afford to buy their children new school clothes. Rashad's younger sisters wore hand-me-downs and Rashad wore his cousin Ramon's clothes from the previous year. Since Ramon attended the same school, Rashad knew that his classmates recognized Ramon's clothing.

Rashad felt mortified to wear those clothes. Did everything in his life have to change so drastically? Rashad felt so humiliated that he could not confront his friends at school. He was sure that his classmates were talking about his family.

His sisters were disruptive in school, and they even fought on the playground. Rashad was embarrassed because everyone could see how poorly his sisters were coping.

Rashad had no life of his own. After school he watched over his sisters. He also fixed dinner so his mother would not need to worry about cooking after she arrived home from work.

By October, Rashad decided that it would be better for everyone if he stopped going to school, and he returned home each morning after walking his sisters to school. That way he could get a few things done around the house. He also needed a break from his sisters and their constant squabbling.

Rashad was attempting to cope with a difficult situation. He, his sisters, and his parents struggled to adjust to a major family transition. But what did other people see and think?

Myths and stereotypes about divorce might suggest several observations: that Rashad's father had abandoned his family; that his sisters' behavior was a result of a "broken home"; and that Rashad was a school dropout whom no one cared about.

Had Rashad's father really abandoned his family, or was he working long hours to support two households? Were Rashad's sisters just "bad kids from a broken home" or were their fights a reaction to the confusion children feel when they do not understand why both parents no longer live with them?

When the stress at home became too great, Rashad could not function at school and dropped out. Would someone understand that Rashad was overwhelmed by his family's transition? Would Rashad develop better coping skills?

Rashad might have benefited by discussing his problems with a trusted adult. If his parents or other relatives were too stressed to listen, Rashad could have confided in his school counselor. Keeping his anger and embarrassment bottled up inside did not give Rashad a chance to deal successfully with the changing circumstances in his life.

Although Rashad was coping as well as he knew how, he made a poor decision by dropping out of school. Keeping busy with class assignments and discussing his concerns openly with his friends could have provided Rashad with an outlet for his frustration.

FAMILY STATISTICS

In earlier generations, divorce was rare. Remarriage usually resulted from the death of a spouse. The new stepparent was someone who "stepped in" to take the role of the deceased family member and acted as a replacement.

Children born in 1900 had a 22-percent chance of experiencing the death of a parent during childhood. Only about 5 percent of children born at the turn of the century had parents who were divorced.

Current statistics estimate that half of the children born in the United States in the 1990s will experience some type of disruption of their nuclear families. But unlike children born ninety years ago, most family upheavals will not result from the death of a parent.

First marriages currently have about a 40-percent chance of ending in divorce. But this does not mean that divorced people have given up on marriage; the remarriage rate is quite high. Usually within three years of a divorce, 75 percent of women and 80 percent of men remarry. Unfortunately, the divorce rate for these remarriages is even higher than the rate for first marriages. About 60 percent of remarriages end in divorce.

Because of the high rates of divorce and remarriage, it is estimated that by the year 2000 the blended family will be the most common form of family.

Most of us find it difficult enough to live harmoniously in a traditional family. In a blended family, living harmoniously takes a greater effort on everyone's part.

While today's blended families often have to work to find acceptance in society, these kinds of families in the near future may find ready acceptance by virtue of their sheer numbers. If current trends continue, the family of the future will be patterned very much like current blended families. Sociologists have predicted that in the twenty-first century it will be normal for families to include a mixture of children by different marriages.

Even if blended families do become the basis for our family structure, it is hard to imagine that the formation of such a family will become easier. Family transition is rarely easy.

The transition and change that young people face during the death or divorce of a parent can be emotionally staggering. Feelings of loss and confusion can be overwhelming. Often family members feel isolated and unsure where they belong. Families need to learn new coping skills to deal with and accept the emotions surrounding death and divorce. In addition to family support, community support can also help young people to let go of their old habits and ideas so that they can learn to accept the way things are.

Just as with divorce or death in a family, the formation of a new family can create a period of transition that is unsettling. Belonging to two families can leave young people feeling uncertain and anxious. When young people move into new households, they often balk at new rules and feel divided loyalties between the present and absent parents.

Young people aren't the only ones confused by new roles when a blended family is created. Stepparents find it hard to forge new relationships with stepchildren who visit only on weekends. Battles concerning money and discipline often make a stepparent unsure of his or her position in the blended family. The transition to becoming a blended family is easier when stepparents don't try to replace biological parents. Cooperation among all of the parents and stepparents will foster a sense of family and demonstrate that respect and consideration for one another are the basic ingredients of any kind of family.

Research shows that 7,000 new blended families form every week. The information and support available to these blended families is growing and improving at a steady rate as well. There are many organizations and support groups that help blended families target and solve their problems.

The best way to help blended families is to reach them at the beginning stages. By learning what to expect, the family can prevent problems from getting out of control. A blended family can learn which problems are temporary and part of the transition, and which problems need more attention and work to solve.

The following guidelines can help to address some of the main issues that a blended family faces. Being aware of these guidelines can help you and your family ease the transition, and help you understand the reasons behind some of the problems. Learning the point of view of your other family members will help you be more sympathetic to their issues, and in turn help your family members be more sympathetic to you.

— It's easy for your parents to get caught up in their new romance and forget the needs of you and your siblings. You need attention and discipline in a new blended family. But also try to understand that your new parents need time together as well.

— Your newly remarried parent and his or her spouse need guidance in their co-parenting responsibilities. By learning how to work together as a team, they will be better able to cope with problems between themselves as well as problems within the new family structure. This guidance will help to smooth out common obstacles that you and your family may encounter.

— Communication is the most important factor. A family that is open and honest leads to better understanding. In order for blended families to succeed, it's necessary for the members of the family to welcome and accept diversity and understand each other. Often a successsful blended family is stronger than a traditional one because of the obstacles they've had to overcome.

If young people living in blended families could wave a magic wand, what would they wish for their families? Some might wish for their biological parents to reunite.

Others might wish for a smoother relationship with a step-parent or stepsibling. But at the base of all the wishes would be what every family hopes for: to have a harmonious family life in which all members are treated with respect and affection.

CHAPTER 2

Divorce as a Cause of Blended Families

Family life has always included tension and conflict. As we have learned, nearly half of all first marriages now end in divorce. Were couples in the past better able to cope with conflict? Are more people divorcing now because they are too lazy to work on problems in their relationships?

Some social scientists believe that the increase in the divorce rate today is due to changes in society's structure. They do not believe that the high divorce rate is caused by the inability of today's couples to work through their differences.

Imagine an unhappy couple in 1950. Their choices were limited. With the shortage of well-paying jobs, a woman in 1950 had few options for supporting herself and her children if she were to divorce her husband.

Fewer birth control methods were available before the 1960s and larger families were the rule rather than the exception. The husband in this case would have anticipated supporting or abandoning a number of children if he were to divorce his wife.

Community and religious influences were strongly against divorce in the 1950s. Since people did not move around as much then, the community and place of worship played greater roles in their decision-making. These two factors would have provided an unhappy couple with yet another reason to attempt to solve their problems.

Consider how options have changed for couples in unhappy marriages today. Many women are able to find jobs to support themselves. This earning power enables women to leave unhappy marriages and still provide for their children as they find satisfaction in their lives.

Today, couples have access to birth control methods to provide them with choices about family size. Although divorce still is not viewed as a positive choice by many, it does not carry the same stigma that it once did. Due to these changes, many communities have become more tolerant of divorce, although many churches and synagogues still are not.

While death, divorce, single parenthood, and abandonment all disrupt the nuclear family, divorce is the most common reason for family dissolution. No two divorces are the same, and each mother, father, and child experiences the process of divorce differently.

How do young people experience divorce? The age of the child involved determines how much he or she can understand. Feelings of fear, sadness, anger, and loss are common. The severity and extent of these feelings depend on how the parents respond to their child before, during, and after the divorce.

Are your parents divorced? Divorce has become so common that more than one-third of all children today can answer yes to this question.

Americans should not be surprised that divorce is so common. A divorce is easier and quicker for parents to obtain in the United States than in any other country in the West, except Sweden. All fifty states allow couples to divorce because the marriage has collapsed. No one needs to be blamed. No one needs to be at fault.

Many states permit divorce after a couple has been separated for one year. A divorce is granted even if only one spouse wants the divorce and the other spouse is not at fault.

By contrast, couples in England must wait five years for a divorce if one partner objects to the divorce. In France, couples must wait six years, and the court may not grant a divorce if it would result in great hardship for a reluctant wife or her children.

Although the United States permits quick and easy divorce, our laws do little to ensure that both parents will continue to support their children. According to U.S. Census Bureau surveys, only about half of all fathers who are ordered by the court to pay child support actually pay the full amount.

BEFORE THE DIVORCE

— "Your mom has fallen in love with someone else."
— "Mom has been very depressed for a long time and has decided that she can no longer take care of you. She can barely take care of herself."
— "Your father has beaten me for the last time. This is not how a family should get along."

The reasons for divorce are endless. A parent addicted to alcohol may cause one family to fall apart. Another family may be able to function with an alcoholic member and choose to stay intact.

Whatever the reason, a divorce signals the beginning of change—a period of family transition. It indicates change from a two-parent to a single-parent household.

For parents with marriage problems, divorce may seem like an end to a problem rather than a transition. A divorce may remove a violent spouse from the home or end emotional suffering. But viewed through a child's eyes, divorce often seems less like an end and more like the beginning of a number of family changes.

Chet's Story

Chet had just started middle school when his parents divorced. When Chet's mother finally told him that she and his father were splitting up, Chet tried to keep a positive attitude.

Ever since he could remember, Chet had seen his parents argue. They rarely agreed on anything. They often even fought over how to fix dinner or complete other daily chores.

Sometimes Chet's father would disappear for weeks at a time after he and Chet's mother had argued. These were periods of peace and quiet for Chet, his younger sister, Emily, and their mother.

Chet's mother explained that the divorce would be a new beginning for her. Since she and his father could not get along, she saw divorce as a chance to raise Chet and Emily in a more tranquil environment.

Chet's father planned to live nearby so that Chet and Emily could spend part of each week with him and part of the week with their mother. Chet's parents decided that this arrangement was best for the family. They felt that divorce was the only way to put an end to their fighting.

While Chet understood his parents' needs, he was angry. Couldn't his parents find another way to stop their fighting? He also worried about what might happen to him and Emily if his parents didn't stop fighting *after* the divorce.

UNDERSTANDING DIVORCE

Even when homes are filled with tension, most children want their families to stay together. To some children, life in a stressful family seems better than life with a single parent.

A family should provide children with stability, support, and continuity in what is often an unpredictable world. When families become unstable, children become frightened. While they may notice changes, many children try not to think about what it means when their parents start to behave differently. To cope with their fear, they bury their feelings and accept the problem as normal.

Children do not have a lifetime of experience to help them sort out their parents' behavior. They assume that their families are permanent and that they will be safe within them.

Even young children have an idea of how people meet, fall in love, and marry. But how people divorce is vague, unfamiliar, and sometimes violent. Before they decide to divorce, many parents try to hide their problems from the children to save them some of the pain that they themselves are experiencing.

Some parents are afraid that their children will not understand what is happening. Children also may try to persuade their parents to reconcile, making the entire decision more painful. Another reason that children often are not told about the possibility of divorce is that many parents try to stay together for the sake of the children. Many parents feel guilty that their children will suffer just so they can improve their own lives. Some parents endure a number of separations and reconciliations because they try staying together for the children.

Children need to be able to trust their family unit and feel secure with it. Many researchers and mental health professionals believe that divorce may be preferable to living in a family that is in constant conflict.

Can you imagine how it might be better to have divorced parents rather than married parents?

Consider these examples:

- Your best friend's father and mother fight over everything. The father often ends their arguments by physically abusing his wife and storming out of the house. Your friend is so upset after these fights that he cannot cope with his schoolwork or with many of your mutual friends. Your friend seems to be depressed all the time.

Studies show that young people are better adjusted when living in single-parent families without conflict than in dysfunctional intact families. How can these parents decide if their problems are too big to solve?

Do you think your friend would be better off living in a conflict-free family? Should his mother insist that her husband leave even if your friend loves his father and wants him to stay? Will the mother feel too guilty to proceed with the divorce?

- Your cousin has told you that her parents sleep in separate rooms, but she is not sure what that means. She hopes that it is just because her father snores. You overhear your aunt telling your mother that her marriage is finished but that they are going to remain together until your cousin is a little older.

Research suggests that conflict between parents is more damaging to children the longer it continues, the more openly hostile it becomes, and the more it focuses on the children. Is it right for parents to hide their true feelings from their children? Whom does that benefit? Is it better that your aunt and uncle are waiting until your cousin is older to divorce, or would it be better for everyone if they divorced now? These are hard questions to answer. Each family must work to decide what is the best solution for them.

AFTER THE DIVORCE: WHAT MAKES A DIFFERENCE?

The first two years after a divorce are usually the hardest for the family. Watching your parents separate is scary. After seeing that your parents cannot solve their problems, you may find yourself questioning your future. Perhaps the parent you now live with is still depressed over the divorce.

Within two or three years after a divorce, most single parents and their children do recover from the initial trauma. Parents are able to balance their lives as the wounds from the breakup begin to heal. Most children are able to function in their new surroundings.

Janet's Story

My parents divorced three years ago. Right now, I prefer living with my father, but because my parents have joint custody, I stay with my mother about half of the time. I love both of my parents; it's just that it is easier for me to feel good about myself when I live with my father.

My mother stills talks about the divorce, and I think she still is depressed. I feel sorry for her, but I'm not sure why. She agreed to the divorce, and I think she had a certain idea of what life would be like after it happened. Maybe things just didn't turn out the way she planned.

All of my friends who have divorced parents live with their mothers, and they think that my family is weird. I know that most mothers become the custodial parent after a divorce. I am upset that my friends don't understand why I prefer living with my father. Since my parents' divorce, I've become more tolerant of how other families live.

Just after the divorce, I used to wish that my parents would patch things up. My parents have always been friendly to one another, so I thought that maybe they would come to their senses and get back together. But once I realized that my father was happy living on his own, it did not seem so important for my parents to reconcile.

If I could get my parents back together, would I? No, I don't think so. I'm accustomed to the way things are now, and I think that my parents are better off living apart from one another.

I have grown up faster than I think I should have, but I realize that life does not always work out the way you plan. Now I appreciate my parents as individuals. They went through a lot of pain with their divorce and they had to be very strong. I wouldn't want them to endure that pain again if they got back together and it didn't work out.

Janet has accepted her parents' divorce. She now views her family as a group of individuals. Families must learn to cope with the strain of divorce if they are to grow in the future. Some stumbling blocks that families experience after a divorce are the following:

Confusion. Be certain you understand why your parents divorced. Children sometimes feel that the parents are also divorcing them, and they feel intensely rejected. If possible, have both parents explain the reasons together. If a parent remarries, ask that parent how it will affect you.

Sadness. Divorce is a sad event and can cause anxieties that last a long time. Some children imagine that they have caused the divorce. If your parents are too upset with the failure of their marriage to respond to you, talk to someone who is a bit removed from your family. An aunt, an uncle, a school counselor, or a close neighbor may be able to help you. Ask your parents how they cope with their sadness. Even years later, the sadness you feel from your parents' divorce may recur when one of your parents remarries.

Plans for the Future. Plans for your future may seem less certain after a divorce. If you will be moving and changing schools, get the details. If a parent remarries, make it clear that you want to stay involved.

DOES DIVORCE CAUSE PERMANENT EMOTIONAL DAMAGE TO THE CHILDREN?

What if two years pass and children still don't feel good about their family? Sadly, many young people do not cope well with their families' changes even two years after a divorce. A young person may have trouble trusting people and may constantly question other relationships. Does this mean that he or she is scarred for life?

There is no way to know how many children suffer long-term harm from their parents' divorces. But with help, such as counseling and support groups, most young people are able to accept their family circumstances and avoid any permanent emotional suffering.

Parents initiate divorce, and parents have a responsibility to help their children accept the transition. How the custodial parent functions after the divorce greatly determines how well the children learn to cope with the divorce.

Parents may not be ready to take charge as single parents. They may have their own distress and use most of their energy to take care of themselves. Children may have to cope with disorganized schedules, inconsistent discipline, and unclear boundaries.

Unfortunately, the early transition period of divorce is when children need the most help and guidance from their parents. The longer a parent is unable to cope with his or her sadness and loss, the harder the divorce will be on the children of the family.

Calvin's Story

Soon after my parents' divorce, my mother refused to get out of bed. She claimed she just could not face getting up. When she did come out of her room, she was drunk. Since I am fifteen, I took over as many responsibilities as I could. I fed my younger brothers breakfast and made sure that they got to the bus stop on time. Then I went to school.

My grandmother helped out, too. She brought over groceries and kept us company for a while in the evenings. But she could not do everything. After a month, she called the child welfare department and reported my mother.

Boy, was I relieved! My grandmother is too old to be shopping and coming over every day. I worried that she would get sick from all the work. We really needed some help.

My relief didn't last long when I found out what would happen next. My younger brothers and I were going to be placed in foster care. I would be sent alone to a family who would care for me until my mother got better. My brothers would be sent together to a family who could care for both of them. This was the first time that I had ever been separated from my family. I was terrified.

I didn't stay with my foster family very long. I couldn't wait until my mother got better. I knew that might be a very long time. My foster family treated me well, but their concern seemed so fake. My own family had just broken up, and I could not stand to see another family acting so happy. So I left. I ran away.

But I did not want to go to my grandmother since she had called the authorities in the first place. None of my friends' parents would let me stay with them when they found out that I had run away. I didn't have anywhere else to go, since my father had moved far away.

I spent most of my time on the streets or hanging out in the park. Occasionally, I would sneak into my mother's house after she turned off the lights and sleep in my old bed, but only if the weather was really bad. Staying there reminded me of too many sad things.

Calvin may have lasting emotional problems from his parents' divorce. His mother was unable to cope with her alcoholism, and she failed to provide support for her children.

When left to sort through their parents' divorce alone, young people often face depression, poor grades at school, lowered self-esteem, and mental confusion.

When a couple divorces, it is the beginning of a time of transition for their family. If your family has been through a divorce, you are not alone. As many as two out of every five marriages today ends in divorce.

Calvin had other options available to him. Running away from his foster family didn't help him cope with his problems. He could have confided in his foster parents, and given them a chance, or he could have consulted with the social worker and asked to be placed in another family. As it stands, Calvin is living on the streets and risking his education and his future. He would benefit by staying in school and working with social services to help him find a family with whom he feels comfortable living.

Like many other teens, you may be having a hard time getting over your parents' divorce. Depending on the circumstances, or how your parents behave, you may have many issues to face. But as many teens have discovered, the pain of divorce lessens with time. As you struggle to find a new kind of life with your mom and dad, try to remember: You may be angry with your parents right now, but you have only one father and one mother. You need their love and support, and they need yours, too.

Try not to focus on who was to blame for the divorce. Many people may be ready to blame either your mother or your father for what happened. One of your parents may blame the other for the divorce. But you don't know all the reasons for what happened. It's best to try and avoid taking sides. Let your parents know that you don't want to take sides if they encourage you to do so.

You are not to blame for your parents' divorce. Divorce, like marriage, is between the two people involved.

Talk to your parents about your feelings. Let them know when and why you feel sad or angry.

Try to understand that, like you, your parents are trying to build new lives. They may begin dating other people. They may even remarry someday.

Above all, remember that you are not alone. Many teens have gone through the pain of their parents' divorce. And many people who understand what you are going through are ready to help you. All you have to do is reach out to them. They can help you find ways to deal with your pain in positive ways. Then you can put the divorce behind you and begin to look toward the future with hope.

CHAPTER 3

Blended Families After the Death of a Parent

"My father had a fatal heart attack while he was at work. He died before he reached the hospital. I still can't believe it. He always seemed so healthy."

"I have many nice memories of my mother. Even though I was only five when she died, my older sisters tell me what she was like, and we have many photographs."

"My father died of emphysema when I was twelve years old. He had been sick for four years. Until three months before his death, he lived at home and my mother and I took care of him. Sometimes I still forget that he is gone, and I wonder if it is time to give my father his medicine."

Death changes the family structure. The family will never be the same after the death of a parent. The way a family reacts to and eventually recovers from the loss of a parent depends on many factors.

How did the death occur? Was it expected? Did the adults involved allow the children to express their sadness? Was the surviving parent able to cope with his or her loss? The success of the future single-parent family or blended family depends on how the surviving family members cope.

Today, when a parent dies, the surviving spouse generally lives with his or her children in a single-parent family. When there is no surviving parent, or the surviving parent is unable to care for the children, relatives or advocates from the state welfare system find foster homes for the children.

ADJUSTMENT TO THE LOSS OF A PARENT

Renée's Story

Although it was nearly three years ago, Renée remembers the day her mother died so clearly that it could have been this morning. That day began just like any other day for Renée. Her mother was rushing around, trying to leave for work on time while urging Renée and her sister, Alyssa, to get ready for the school bus.

Thinking back, Renée still finds it hard to accept that what seemed like such an ordinary day would be the end of her life as she knew it. At lunch time, her mother was crossing the street in front of the beauty parlor where she worked. She was killed instantly when a car sped through a red light and hit her. Renée couldn't believe that just because someone was careless and in a rush, her mother was dead.

After all this time, Renée remembers the shock and disbelief she felt when her aunt picked her up at school that day and told her what had happened. Renée still thinks of her mother every day, but she doesn't cry as often anymore.

Renée's father has not recovered from the loss. He never talks about his wife, and he has not even cleared out her closet or dresser.

Her father's lack of communication still upsets Renée. Since her mother's death, her father hardly talks to anyone. All he seems to do is watch television and drink beer. Renée almost feels as if she has lost her father, too. He certainly is not the same person he used to be before her mother died.

Renée and Alyssa try to be cheerful around their father. That isn't easy, but it seems to be what their dad expects. Alyssa never openly expressed her emotions after her mom died, so Renée never asked Alyssa how she felt. Renée and Alyssa never mention their mother to each other. Renée is afraid that talking about their mom might upset Alyssa. Renée still hears Alyssa crying in her room at night.

In the last three years, there were so many things Renée wondered about, things that she never had the chance to ask her mother. What would Mom have thought in certain situations? What was Mom like when Renée was a baby? How did Mom choose her career?

There were other things that Renée couldn't remember as clearly as she wished. Her mom always seemed so happy, but was she? Did she ever feel sad or have regrets about her life?

Renée hoped that someday her dad would be able to talk about her mother and answer some of her questions. But for now, Renée did not ask him. He seemed so sad and depressed all the time. And Renée felt the same way.

The reality of a sudden death is hard for all families to accept. The death of Renée's mother left a deep void in her family's life. Unfortunately, Renée's father seemed unable to cope with the shock and anger of his loss.

The surviving parent's adjustment to the death of a spouse will greatly affect the response of the children in the family. Renée and Alyssa are still mourning their mother's death three years later. Until their father can successfully grieve for his wife, he will be unable to help his children heal their emotional wounds.

There is no set time limit for grieving. During the early stages of mourning a parent's or spouse's death, people may suffer from physical problems. Loss of appetite, nausea, or compulsive eating and drinking are not uncommon. Moodiness and depression also often occur. If intense grieving continues beyond a few months or a year, as in Renée's family, it is best to seek counseling.

Young people need to be able to express their grief. If ignored, they often bury their feelings, only to have them surface at a later time. Alyssa's response was to grieve alone in her room. Not only did Alyssa lose her mother, but she also lost the support of her father.

Renée also needed her father's support. Without his guidance, she was unable to understand her feelings and memories about her mother.

To grieve successfully, children must be allowed to feel sadness, depression, and anger. Only then will they begin to accept their loss and have a chance to grow emotionally.

Christine's Story

Christine was tired. Her father's funeral was four weeks ago today. Now all Christine wanted was for her life to calm down. The plane crash had been on the local news, so it was no secret at school that her father was dead.

"I was embarrassed when I returned to school," ten-year-old Christine explained. "*Everybody* knew that my father had died. Even kids who weren't in the fifth grade knew. That made me angry. I don't think my father's death is everybody's business."

Relatives were still calling and dropping by every day to visit Christine's family. Christine didn't feel like crying as often now as when her father had first died. But when she did cry, it was hard to find any privacy in her own house. Someone was always there, delivering a casserole or talking to her mother.

Even the children at school treated her differently. At first none of the kids in her class would talk to her. After a few days, they started to loosen up. A few of her friends even sent sympathy cards. But they still treated her differently. They were too nice. Christine did not want to be treated differently.

Ms. Chavez, Christine's school counselor, suggested that her classmates' behavior was due to embarrassment. Her peers could not imagine what it would be like to lose their fathers. She also reminded Christine that she would not feel so angry and sad forever. She told Christine that in time she probably would appreciate her classmates' concern.

Christine was angry at her father for disturbing her life so much. She wondered if things would ever settle down. Ms. Chavez explained that often, it takes a family years to adjust to the death of a parent. While anger is a normal and natural reaction after the death of a parent, Christine will need to learn how to express her anger in healthy ways in order to cope with her new circumstances.

Ms. Chavez was able to help Christine understand some of her anger and the changes in her life. She provided Christine with a sympathetic ear and suggestions about coping with her grief.

Besides talking with a school counselor, people may turn to professionals in their churches or synagogues. Talking to peers who also have experienced the death of a parent is often helpful.

Unlike Christine, who knew all about her father's death, many children are shielded from the truth. The surviving parent may feel that the facts are too upsetting. These parents prefer to let the child learn about the death gradually.

Yet even small children sense that something is wrong if told that their mother is sick or has taken a long trip. Parents mean well by not telling the truth immediately, but children often end up with feelings of abandonment and a poor understanding of death. It is best for families to share their feelings of grief.

- "Did you see how Aunt Selma cried at Dad's funeral? I was so embarrassed," complained eleven-year-old Dwayne.
- "I knew that Mom was sick, but I got so upset at the wake. I think I should have been told what to expect," said nine-year-old Rosa.

Children ages nine to twelve often show a wide variation in their response to death. One minute, preteens will act mature and understanding about the situation. Later the same day, they may be more concerned about their appearance or how to behave when company arrives.

By the time a child moves into the teenage years, he or she probably will have many of the same emotions that adults feel concerning death. Yet it is unlikely that they will have adult coping skills.

A teenager's emotions concerning death may be childlike and hysterical one minute, only to be followed by embarrassed laughter the next minute as the young adult tries to establish an adult response. A teenager's whole belief system may be put into question as he or she tries to come to terms with the anguish of losing a parent.

A teenager has already begun to rely on people other than parents to shape his or her world. Many older teens have outside support opportunities for their grief. Friends, teachers, and relatives may help console teenagers following the death of a parent.

There are also support groups for teenagers who have lost a parent to death. School counselors or social workers from your local hospital can put you in touch with nearby groups. While many people are reluctant to share their feelings with a group of strangers, most people experience the same stages of grief and can be helped by others who are going through the same process.

Bella

Bella, the youngest of three children, was a college freshman when her father died. Her brother called her late one evening in September and reported that their father had suffered a fatal heart attack.

Although Bella's father had seemed fairly stable when she left for school the previous month, during the past five years he had experienced two near-fatal attacks. Even so Bella couldn't believe that he was gone so suddenly. As she made plane reservations for the trip home, she was numb with shock and denial.

"Why did it have to be my father?" Bella asked herself over and over as she stared out the window of the plane. "I should have tried to help him more. Maybe if I had forced him to take better care of himself, he would still be alive."

Bella's "bargaining" lasted the entire flight home, until she met her sister at the airport when she landed. When someone dies, it's often difficult to accept that we have no control over death. Bargaining makes us think we could have done something to stop it. By taking some responsibility for the death, we try to regain control.

As Bella stepped into her sobbing sister's arms, Bella broke down and cried uncontrollably for the first time. Her father had died, and she had not even had a chance to tell him goodbye.

As her sister drove to their parents' home, Bella felt as if she were a zombie. She listened as her sister described that last trip their father made to the hospital and explained the funeral arrangements. But Bella could not concentrate on her sister's words. She felt tired and detached. She again felt numb with shock.

Bella was so depressed that she was not much comfort to her mother, who talked constantly about her husband's last days. In fact, Bella spent much of the week lying down in the bedroom just to escape the idle chatter of their many visitors in the days after the funeral.

When Bella returned to college the following week, she still could not concentrate. All she thought about were incidents from her childhood. Images of her father hovered in her mind both while she was awake and while she tried to sleep.

When Bella returned home two months later for Thanksgiving, she found her family's relationships had changed drastically. Her brother and sister-in-law prepared the traditional Thanksgiving meal, which their mother, Bella, her sister, her brother-in-law, and all the grandchildren attended.

But the holiday was a dismal, uncomfortable affair. There was little conversation other than minimal pleasantries. Even the youngsters sat quietly and ate without speaking to one another.

Family gatherings as Bella remembered them would never be the same, and two months simply was too soon to share a family celebration. The loss of their loved one was just too painful for the surviving family members. They needed more time to establish a new set of guidelines for observing holidays.

Bella returned to college after the long weekend, dreading her winter vacation from school. She knew her mother expected her to return home then, but Bella's depression had deepened during the Thanksgiving break. She did not want to endure such pain again so soon.

Apparently the rest of Bella's family felt the same. A week later, Bella's mom called her at school.

"My sister in Tucson invited you and me to spend Christmas with them," Bella's mom blurted out with more enthusiasm than she'd shown since before her husband's death. "You've always enjoyed Maggie and her kids. Shall we do it?"

"Yes, Mom. Let's!" Bella didn't hesitate to respond. "The change of scenery will be good for both of us."

"That's what I thought," Bella's mom answered. "It will be wonderful to get away for a while."

During the following year, Bella and her mother managed to spend most holidays together, but not in the same manner as in previous years. As the months slipped by they found themselves reminding each other of happy times they had shared with Bella's father.

Bella often felt like crying when she and her mother talked, but afterward she was comforted by her positive memories. She even became accustomed to the tears her mother usually shed, knowing that her mother, too, benefited by acknowledging their loss.

Bella's sister and her family and her brother and his family also established new ways of observing

holidays. The remaining family no longer came together for large family celebrations.

By changing the family's traditions, Bella and her
mother were able to move on to the next phase of
their lives. They remembered the good times, but
were able to try new experiences.

During Bella's third year of college, she started
to date again. Bella's mother also started to date.
Because Bella had been able to share so much with
her mother during the months following her father's
death, it wasn't hard for the two to share many of
their ideas about dating.

By the time Bella's mother remarried two years
later, Bella and her siblings were ready to accept their
new stepfather and stepsister. Though Bella still
missed her father, time and new traditions helped her
realize that the creation of her new blended family
would have made her father proud.

Time is usually a great healer to those who mourn. It is
important to grieve openly and discuss your loss with
others who understand. A picture, a memento, or a shared
memory is often a comfort that may gently remind you of
happier times with your deceased parent.

The pain and sadness following the death of a parent
takes time to accept. A parent who dies will never be for-
gotten, and no one should ever try to replace her or him.
But it is possible for children and young adults to experience the loss of a parent and still form successful relationships in the future. Forging new relationships does
not mean you are replacing the absent parent. No one
can replace your parent, but you can still enjoy life and
develop new relationships.

Constructively expressed emotions and support from family and friends help to place the loss of a parent in perspective. Surviving family members can respect the memory of their loved one while moving on with their lives.

CHAPTER 4

Creation of a Blended Family

As we have seen, blended families are different from nuclear families. Yet the nuclear family is the only positive model for parental roles and family relationships that most of us know. As blended families grow in number, it is to be hoped that they will provide more diverse role models.

When a group of people becomes a blended family, the members need time to establish emotional and physical bonds. Family members must respond to many personal circumstances with compromise and creativity. At the same time, they must establish new rules for themselves and revise their concepts of what constitutes a family.

CHALLENGES FOR NEWLY BLENDED FAMILIES

The basic needs of everyday life for reorganized families vary from the trivial to the enormous. Children traveling between two households need duplicate supplies, everything from toothpaste to clothing. Parents need flexible work schedules to plan their time off around custody considerations. Health insurance and legal rights for blended families are also not as clear-cut as they are for nuclear families.

These examples illustrate some basic problems faced by blended families:

- Austin's parents divorced when he was an infant. Now seven years old, Austin lives with his biological father and his father's partner, Wyatt. Austin's father and Wyatt have shared a household for more than six years. Wyatt has always treated Austin as his own biological son and taken an active role in Austin's life.

  During an average week, Wyatt picked up Austin from school and helped him with his homework. On the weekend, Wyatt and Austin attended a karate class together. They both hoped to attain black belt level before Austin was ten years old.

  But in order for Wyatt to provide medical care for Austin in an emergency, he had to have a signed medical authorization form. Wyatt felt angry and embarrassed that he had to carry a permission slip in order to treat Austin as his son.

- With financial aid, Tasha knew that she would be able to afford college if she also worked nights as a waitress. But when Tasha applied for financial aid, her application was rejected. Tasha was surprised since her primary parent, her mother, had no savings. Tasha's mother earned just enough for the two of them to live on.

Since her parents' divorce ten years ago, Tasha had lived exclusively with her mother. She saw her father only once a year when he attended an annual sales meeting in nearby Boston. Her father had remarried a woman with three children and moved away.

Tasha's father's second family demanded most of his attention and resources. As a result, he showed little emotional or financial interest in Tasha, though he did retain joint custody over her.

Because her father was jointly responsible for her well-being, the college examined her father's tax returns when considering Tasha's eligibility for funding. When the college found out how much her father earned, Tasha was disqualified as a funding recipient. Tasha knew that her father was legally bound by the custody agreement to support her, but she could not force him to pay for her college expenses.

Marshal and Rayleen's Story

Marshal married Rayleen soon after his wife had died. At the time, Marshal's sons, Eric and Paul, were two and six years old. The boys loved their step-mother and felt secure in their family. Rayleen enjoyed her new status as a parent, but there was a problem.

Paul had been born with cystic fibrosis and as a result, he often missed school. Rayleen wanted to help Paul and stay home from work when he needed her. But Rayleen's supervisor felt this was against company policy. A stepson was not her "real" son.

"You can't miss work to take care of someone who is not a blood relative," her supervisor said. "If you do, other employees might request time off to help friends or other distant relatives."

Without Rayleen's help, Marshal became overworked caring for Paul by himself. Paul couldn't understand why his stepmother could not stay home to help him. Didn't she love him enough?

Blended families must struggle to find solutions for basic needs like health insurance and paid time off to care for a family member. They also must constantly adjust their personal roles and values concerning family life.

Should the children call their stepfather "Dad," "Stepdad," or by his first name? How can a fourteen-year-old boy accept a new, younger halfbrother when he has always been the "baby" in his family? Will an energetic three-year-old be accepted into her adoptive parent's extended family? How will it feel the first time Mom comes over after Dad and Jeanie get married?

With so many constantly changing issues, it is no wonder that slightly more than half of all remarriages end in divorce. Dealing with challenges realistically as they occur can help a newly formed family work toward the creation of a harmonious blended family.

EXPECTATIONS AND REALITIES

Do you have a best friend? Did you know that he or she would become your best friend the first time you met each other? How long did it take before you became best friends?

Love and friendship cannot be forced. Experts suggest that it takes from three to five years for a new family to break down the barriers that prevent members from developing positive feelings toward each other.

Parents and children arrive in their new families with expectations of family life that usually are based on past experience. A primary task of members in a new family is to learn how to revise their basic assumptions about family life.

Disappointments result when adults anticipate that an emotionally close family will develop immediately. Different sets of stepchildren may be expected to cooperate too soon. Sometimes a stepparent without previous experience in parenting hopes to forge close ties with a rebellious teenager. All of these relationships take time and cannot successfully be rushed.

Children also enter new families with emotional expectations. When they have experienced the death of a parent, children may vow not to let a stepparent get close, in order to preserve the memory of the deceased parent.

Other children who have lived in a single-parent family for many years may promise themselves never to trust the stepparent who ruined their lives and forced them to share their parent's attention and love. Still other children may hope for affection that their biological parents did. not provide, only to find a stepparent has other priorities besides parenting.

The expression of closeness and intimacy felt by families often depends on the form of family. Large nuclear families will have a style of intimacy different from a family made up of one parent and one child.

The manner in which family members exhibit their emotions varies. The depth of positive feelings or how emotionally connected the members feel toward one another determines how harmonious life in any family will be.

Since children in blended families often are participating in more than one family, they may feel less emotionally connected to their many family members. A young person's blended family may include two sets of parents, four sets of grandparents, and siblings who live in different houses.

No single family member can fulfill all of his or her family's needs. A relaxed and more flexible level of emotional bonding seems to benefit blended families by allowing members to respond more freely to the different emotional demands they encounter.

Darryl's Story

When Darryl was twenty-five, his older brother, Tom, and Tom's wife were killed in a drive-by shooting. Their children, Mindy, three years old, and Todd, six months old, instantly became orphans.

Darryl's mother, Mindy and Todd's grandmother, wanted to help in any way that she could. But she had to care for her sick husband and was unable to provide a permanent home for her two grandchildren.

Darryl had only recently married and was hesitant to take in two young children. He and his wife had planned to wait for a few years before starting a family. Yet, under the tragic circumstances, he accepted the responsibility even though he worried about the effect it might have on his new marriage. He and his wife, Nula, would adopt the two children and hope for the best.

Both Darryl and Nula worked long hours, so they hired a nanny. Darryl hoped that they would find some other, lower-cost child care later since their budget wasn't really large enough to pay for a full-time nanny.

Mindy, who had been in the car with her parents at the time, remembered the shooting and experienced nightmares for nearly a year. At first, she cried whenever Darryl or Nula left her to go to work. But gradually, Mindy accepted the nanny as a mother figure and adjusted to the change in her life.

Even though the children adjusted to their new surroundings, Darryl and Nula felt frustrated with the constant confusion that accompanied life with two preschool children. While they loved the children, they couldn't adjust their lives fast enough. Nula found the change particularly hard. When she married Darryl, she never imagined that she would be raising children that were not biologically her own.

Darryl finally contacted a local mental health agency. For very little expense, he and Nula worked with a family counselor to ease their transition from a childless couple to a family of four. It took some time, but with patience, practice, and advice from their counselor, Darryl and Nula learned not only to cope with, but also to enjoy their new family.

When parents and children form new families, their new lives also affect grandparents and introduce stepgrandparents. Grandparents and stepgrandparents may also bring a new member into an extended family when they remarry after a divorce or death of a spouse.

When parents form new marriages, the roles of grandparents and stepgrandparents can become confusing. What should a stepgrandparent be called? What happens to grandparents when a custodial parent moves to another state? Some children have two sets of grandparents and two sets of stepgrandparents. Can they get to know all of them?

The roles that grandparents and stepgrandparents in a blended family play depend on individual personalities. Unfortunately, there are no clear models for many blended families to follow when introducing stepgrandparents.

Jaclyn's Story

After Jaclyn's parents divorced, Jaclyn's father disappeared without a trace. Jaclyn's mother, Shirrel, was not surprised. The marriage had been an unhappy one for most of Jaclyn's eleven years. Shirrel was not emotionally upset by her former husband's abandonment. Jaclyn had to admit that she didn't miss him much either. But without his court-appointed child support payments, Shirrel and Jaclyn soon were desperate and became welfare recipients.

Shirrel was enrolled in college and had one year left to complete her nursing degree. She worried that without the degree, she and Jaclyn would remain on public assistance forever.

Shirrel could not do it all. She needed someone to look after Jaclyn for the next year. Then Shirrel could attend classes and work part-time as a nurse's aide. But without help, Shirrel's dream of a better life for herself and Jaclyn would be unattainable.

The only person to turn to was Jaclyn's father's mother, Grandma Mae. Jaclyn did not know her grandmother very well since her father's family had always kept their distance. But now that her son had disappeared and left his family with bills to pay,

Grandma Mae wanted to help. Jaclyn thought that perhaps Grandma Mae felt guilty about her son's behavior.

Jaclyn wasn't happy with the idea of living with her grandmother for a year, but the alternative was to remain on welfare. The first few weeks at Grandma Mae's were hard for Jaclyn. She missed her apartment, and she missed her mother even though they spoke on the phone every night. But Jaclyn soon found that when she was feeling lonely, Grandma Mae was always there to talk. Grandma Mae was lonely, too. Even though she was mad at her son for abandoning his family, she missed him terribly. She and Jaclyn were able to talk about their situation together and become good friends.

During her last year of nursing school, Shirrel started dating Jack, a fellow nursing student. Jack was different from Jaclyn's father in every way. It was no surprise to Jaclyn that Shirrel fell in love with him. Jaclyn was happy to see her mother dating a man who seemed so caring. Shortly before graduation in May, Shirrel told Jaclyn that she planned to marry Jack in July.

Jack's family threw a large party after graduation. They were celebrating both Jack and Shirrel's graduation and engagement. The party was Jaclyn's first time meeting Jack's entire family.

Even though Jack's family was warm and open to Jaclyn, she felt sad. Grandma Mae wasn't included in the celebration. And now, Jack's parents seemed eager to be her new grandparents.

Jaclyn was desperate to not lose Grandma Mae. Grandma Mae couldn't be replaced by Jack's parents, no matter how friendly they were. Jaclyn was so confused that she left the party early and went back to Grandma Mae's house.

Jaclyn found her grandmother waiting for her. Grandma Mae understood that meeting Jack's family was hard. But she reminded Jaclyn that she and her mother had only agreed to let Jaclyn live with Grandma Mae for one year. Their goal was for Shirrel to earn her degree so she could work for a brighter future. Grandma Mae felt that there would be room in Jaclyn's life for two more grandparents.

That night, Jaclyn and her grandmother made a plan. They would meet for dinner at Grandma Mae's house once a week, just the two of them. Knowing that she would have a special time with Grandma Mae helped to calm Jaclyn's nerves. Having a plan gave Jaclyn the confidence to consider what her new family might be like, especially if she didn't have to lose Grandma Mae.

Making plans with relatives, as Jaclyn did with Grandma Mae, is one way to ease the transition towards new family arrangements. But what if your family isn't getting along? Many children are separated from their grandparents when their parents go through an unfriendly divorce.

The rights of grandparents and stepgrandparents are unclear and vary from state to state. Most states have "grandparents' rights organizations" that can give you or your grandparents information on how to blend together with new family members. They can also suggest how to arrange visits if there are bad feelings between divorced parents.

While stepgrandparents have even more unclear rights in regard to stepgrandchildren, the same organizations can provide information for them, too.

WHO ARE YOUR FAMILY MEMBERS?

There are no distinct guidelines for defining family members in blended families. As we have seen, family members often are confused as to how to define their family. Businesses, such as health care providers and college assistance programs, also are not consistent or clear about whom to include.

To succeed in such a situation, family members must be highly adaptable. Unlike nuclear families, family roles, expectations, and members may constantly change in blended families.

In a blended family, members must select their family members from the pool of former spouses and noncustodial parents. Other members may include visiting stepsiblings and former in-laws.

Tyler's Story

Christmas would arrive in exactly one month. It would be the first holiday that Tyler would spend with his mother and new stepfather. His mother and father had always spent Christmas together with Tyler, even after they divorced.

Not only would Tyler not see his father this Christmas, he also would not see his paternal grandparents. Of course, he had seen little of them since his mother married Bryce anyway.

Tyler was uncertain how this first Christmas would turn out. He hoped that Bryce's parents would accept him as a new grandson; they already had three other grandchildren whom they'd known since birth. Bryce's immediate family was small and very close. How long would it take for Tyler to be considered "family"?

Tyler's family had been reshuffled. His father's presence was replaced by Bryce, his stepfather. Bryce's parents were available as grandparents, while at the same time, Tyler saw less of his biological paternal grandparents.

Like Tyler, some children in blended families find themselves in a web of relationships. Little is known about the long-term effects on children's lives from these new patterns of complex family relationships. Research has yet to explore how a third set of grandparents, like Tyler's, will significantly affect a child's future development.

As families move through divorce, death, and remarriage, individuals become related to more and more people. Some families find it easier to adapt when they have a model to follow. After nontraditional families are formed, their members often find that there is no "normal" nontraditional family model established.

Educational/support groups for nontraditional families help people in these situations to understand the realities of blended family life. These groups often are offered by teachers, school counselors, the clergy, and various community organizations.

Louise's Story

The homework for the first week's class seemed silly to Louise: "Write one page describing your idea of the perfect family." Were they kidding?

When her school counselor had told her that the Girl Scouts sponsored a four-week program for children from blended families, Louise had been excited. Her mother had remarried the previous year and moved with Louise and her brother, Logan, to Chicago. Louise would rather be back in Iowa with her grandparents. But instead she was stuck with this weird homework assignment.

Logan was supposed to attend the program with her, which Louise thought even stranger than the assignment. Before the first week's session, she wondered how he would feel going to class with the Girl Scouts. After they arrived, Louise realized that a person did not have to be female or a Girl Scout to attend the program called "Families in Transition."

At the first class, a judge was the featured speaker. The judge explained the rules for awarding custody of children in divorce cases. The speaker in the second class was a young woman not much older than Louise who was a single mother. After each speaker, there was a discussion and then, of course, the homework assignment.

At the end of the four weeks, Louise's original homework assignment was returned to her. She was amazed at how much she had learned about understanding human nature in the class. She had written that the perfect family was a nuclear family who *never* had problems, pressures, or disappointments. Now she knew that her previous expectations were far too idealistic for any family to achieve.

Louise realized that although her family life was not "perfect," with time, understanding and compromise, happiness in a blended family was possible.

DIVIDED LOYALTIES

It is natural to feel that your loyalties belong with your biological parents. You may feel guilty about developing close bonds with a stepparent. But that doesn't mean you love your biological parents any less. Through open communication both you and your parents can learn to accept the new people in your lives. Everyone can come to understand that forming close relationships with new family members is essential to the success of a blended family.

Megan's Story

Megan's parents divorced ten years ago, when she was three years old. Megan's stepmom, Harriet, was exceptionally kind to her. Yet Megan rarely responded in a positive manner.

As the years passed and Harriet was unable to conceive a child of her own, she tried even harder to befriend Megan. But Megan continued to make things difficult whenever she visited her dad and Harriet.

But now, as Megan began to realize how happy Harriet made her father, Megan started to reconsider her actions. And that made her feel guilty.

Megan's mom had never remarried. Although Megan's dad honored his alimony and child support responsibilities, her mother had always needed to work. Until now, Megan resented the vast difference in living style between her mom's house and her father's larger house.

But now she began to enjoy the pool, the large television, and her fancy bedroom at her father's house. She also began to enjoy Harriet's company, and that made Megan feel awful inside.

Was she betraying her mother's love by becoming friendly with Harriet? Why did she feel that she was abandoning her mother when she enjoyed herself at her father's home? Did all children of divorced parents feel this tug of war between their parents?

Megan became frustrated with her new emotions, and she began to avoid Harriet's company when she visited. But that made her angry with her mom for putting her in that awkward position. After several weekend visits to her dad's house, Megan's mother confronted her.

"What are you so unhappy about?" Megan's mother asked. "Did Harriet or your father do something to upset you?"

Megan trusted her mother enough to discuss her feelings. Her mother's reaction surprised Megan.

"Harriet is a nice person," her mom said. "And she has always been nice to you. Now that you're older, it's normal that you appreciate her efforts in making you feel comfortable in their family."

"You aren't hurt?" Megan asked.

"I know you love me, honey," her mother answered. "You are a member of both families, and I'm glad you enjoy your father's new family."

Megan felt enormously relieved after talking with her mother. Megan felt an even greater loyalty to her mother for her willingness to do what she felt best for her daughter. She wondered if many children of divorced parents were as lucky as she was. Megan hoped so.

Megan did the right thing. She talked openly with her mother about her feelings. When she felt divided between her biological mother and her stepmother, she felt guilty all the time. Her feelings were beginning to affect her life in negative ways. Her actions towards her stepmother could have created real problems for her father and their blended family. If Megan continued to resent Harriet, it may have caused a rift between her father and his new wife. But Megan decided to confront the problem and by acting in a responsible way, she helped ease the transition for everyone—including herself.

CHAPTER 5

Stepparents in a Blended Family

Many myths can surround stepparents as they follow parents into their new blended families. You may think stepmothers and stepfathers are mean. You may even think that they are only nice to you so that your biological parent will be happy. As we examine what it is like to be a parent in a blended family, keep in mind that the number of these families continues to increase rapidly. The impact they have on social and legal matters will affect all types of families.

What rights, legal and emotional, does the nonbiological parent have? Is it easier to be a stepmother or a stepfather? Are stepparents happier when their stepchildren live with them or when they just visit? How do stepparents feel when a new baby is born into the stepfamily?

STEPMOTHERS IN A BLENDED FAMILY

When a family separates by divorce, the children usually live with their biological mother full-time or part-time.

The children visit their biological father on weekends or on holidays. As a result, the majority of stepmothers are weekend moms, with stepchildren living with them on a semi–permanent basis.

How a couple divides household duties determines the extent to which visiting stepchildren affect the stepmother's role. The current trend among families is that men do about a third of the domestic work, such as cleaning and cooking. As more women work outside the home, many men have assumed more responsibility in the home.

Even with this increase over time, it is usually the stepmothers who acquire the extra household work when stepchildren visit. In addition to creating extra household duties, visiting stepchildren are just that—they are visiting.

Kate and Karen's Story

Karen and Kate thought their stepmother, Jean, was a very uptight person. She got angry at the smallest things. She seemed to get really upset when they made a mess in the bathroom or borrowed her clothes. Their own mom never minded, but Jean would yell and complain to their father that they were ruining the weekend. It just didn't make sense to Karen and Kate. They had so little time to see their father, Jason. Why spend the weekend helping with housework, or worrying if wet towels were left on the bathroom floor? Their father didn't seem to care too much about Jean's rules, either. He always defended Kate and Karen when Jean complained or yelled at them.

Their father had only asked that they try to be nice to Jean, since he wanted everyone to get along. The girls tried. But nothing seemed to please Jean.

Finally, after dinner one Saturday night, Jean seemed to lose all reason. Karen and Kate had finished dinner and gone into the next room to watch a video. Jean started to yell at their father about his daughters' bad table manners. As usual, Kate and Karen's father had tried to calm Jean down, but she was too mad. She stormed out of the house and refused to return until the girls went back to their mother's house on Sunday afternoon.

Part-time stepchildren can be more stressful than full-time stepchildren. While many stepmothers may not mind the increased domestic work that accompanies visiting children, they often benefit little emotionally. It is not uncommon for fathers to defend visiting children during small family disputes, as with Jason and his daughters.

Visiting stepchildren also place the father in a co-parenting role with the biological mother. Since this may cause the former spouses to renew their emotional attachment, additional strain may be placed on the remarried couple. The stepmother may become uncertain of her role in the new family structure if the biological mother has too much control over the coparenting process.

Because of part-time stepchildren, more housework, and competition from a former wife, many agree that the role of a stepmother is much more difficult than that of a stepfather.

BLENDING WITH A STEPMOTHER

There are ways to make the transition of a new stepmother easier. There are also steps that the family can take together to work toward a harmonious future.

It is generally recognized that younger children will more readily accept a stepmother than older children. Older children often have stronger bonds with the absent parent. They also have their own habits and ways of doing things. Younger children are more flexible in meeting a stepmother's needs. This makes blending with a stepmother easier.

A stepmother also blends into a new family more easily if her natural children live with her. If a stepmother's biological children live elsewhere, the mother often feels guilty raising stepchildren when she cannot raise her own.

A third factor that may ease a stepmother's transition is her attitude. A stepmother who behaves as a concerned adult or as an additional parent will have the least amount of adjustment problems with her stepchildren. A stepmother who wants to be a replacement mother may discover that her stepchildren resent her and resist even her best intentions.

Kirstin's Story

Kirstin is twelve years old with a new stepmother whose children live across the country with their paternal grandparents. Her new stepmother is so upset at the loss of her first family that she is determined to be the world's best mom to Kirstin. But Kirstin doesn't need or want another mother. Her stepmother has only lived with her for six months, yet she has tried to change Kirstin completely.

Kirstin's stepmother has established new rules and even tries to tell her what to wear! Kirstin is stuck in the middle. She can't ask her mother for advice because her mother hates the new stepmom. She can't ask her father because he doesn't think that her stepmother is that bad a mother. None of the factors that usually help a stepfamily to blend is in Kirstin's favor. She needs to look for help.

Experts on stepfamilies offer the following suggestions to help cope with the most common problems of a newly blended family:

- Seek counseling so family problems can be aired in a neutral location. Family counseling would provide a place for Kirstin to explain her problem to her father.
- Discipline must be consistent. Not only was Kirstin's stepmother in charge of discipline, she also was trying to change Kirstin by selecting her clothes. Family counselors suggest that the biological parent should handle discipline, especially in the beginning.
- Build a cooperative relationship with the absent parent. Kirstin's situation would be easier if all of the adults would cooperate.
- Establish open communication. Stepfamilies are encouraged to have regular talk sessions in which everybody can discuss his or her feelings. Since Kirstin's stepmother wanted to be a replacement mother, it was important that she talk about her needs rather than force them on Kirstin.

STEPFATHERS IN A BLENDED FAMILY

Many believe that it is easier to be a stepfather than a stepmother. There is less cultural pressure for men to nurture and care for children. It is more common for children to live with their stepfather and their biological mother on a continual basis, which provides a stage for possible bonding. Yet stepfathers face their own set of problems. Discipline and money are the two most commonly cited hurdles that most stepfathers encounter in their blended families.

Discipline

Even the most sensitive stepfather will hear complaints of injustice from stepchildren if he assumes the role of disciplinarian. A power struggle between stepfather and stepchildren will occur whenever stepfathers try to assume a disciplinary role too quickly.

In response to the turmoil, many stepfathers give up on communicating with their stepchildren and disengage from the stepfather role. After all, they rationalize, I married the mother, not her children.

Children often resent the stepfather's disciplinary role, one previously played by their biological father or mother. A stepfather who assumes too much authority will cause loyalty conflicts for the children. Also, children will not obey someone whom they do not know well or care about. A new stepfather has these two very large hassles to overcome.

In addition to discipline problems, the stepfather often receives mixed messages from his wife. She may want him to share the disciplinary role, but she may be reluctant to actually relinquish any of it. After coping as a single parent, many mothers find it hard to delegate the necessary authority to allow the new husband to share in disciplining her children effectively.

A blended family is most often formed because of the adults' interest in marrying each other, rather than the new spouse's interest in the children. A stepfather who works toward solving severe discipline problems will benefit by strengthening his marriage, which is usually his initial interest. He also should remember that a stepparent does not need to be a replacement parent.

When a stepfather shows respect and courtesy for his stepchildren, the resentment and loyalty conflicts concerning the biological parent are usually lessened. Furthermore, the stepfather will not be placed in the position of needing the children's approval or acceptance as an authority figure.

Rashad's Story

When we first read about Rashad, he had quit school after his parents' divorce. Rashad's decision to stop going to school wasn't working out for him. He felt more lonely than ever and less able to cope with his sisters' disruptive behavior. To make things worse, his mother had started to date someone and seemed to be getting serious with him. This gave Rashad even less time with his mother.

Rashad had no idea how to correct his situation. He was embarrassed that he had stopped attending school but not emotionally ready to admit his mistake. His father was still working long hours. Rashad wished he could see his father more often and tell him how lonely he was. Rashad felt he had no one to talk to.

His mother's boyfriend, Simon, treated Rashad as an adult and didn't try to tell him what to do. He knew that Rashad was not in school, but he never lectured him. Rashad appreciated that Simon wasn't trying to replace his father. Simon actually had a son of his own who was just a few years older than Rashad. When Simon suggested that Rashad and his mother come with him to his son's parents' weekend at college, Rashad was horrified. How could he go to a college weekend when he wasn't even attending high school?

Rashad's mother helped him make up his mind. He could either come to the college weekend or stay at home and take care of his sisters. Rashad quickly decided that a visit to a college would be easier.

Simon's son, Gordon, was in the middle of his first semester of college. Gordon was a lot like his father. He was relaxed and didn't seem to judge people too quickly. Rashad found Gordon easy to talk to, and he quickly learned all about Gordon's move to college. By the end of the weekend, Rashad felt that he had made a new friend.

Gordon spent part of his Christmas break visiting his father. Even though his visit was short, Gordon and Rashad saw a lot of each other. The more Rashad heard about Gordon's college experiences, the more he knew that he was ready to return to school. Rashad had a new goal. He wanted to attend college like Gordon.

Rashad returned to school in January. He was behind in all subjects and had to work most nights and weekends to make up for the lost months. He was also expected to attend summer classes.

In the spring, Rashad's family life changed again. His mother and Simon became engaged. Unfortunately, his sisters did not take the news well. With the engagement announcement, their behavior became so obnoxious that Rashad's mother could not handle it. Rashad's parents decided that the girls would move out to their grandparents' farm. Their father would be able to be with them in the evenings when he finished work. And more importantly, their grandmother would be with them before and after school to give their lives some structure.

If Rashad continued to work hard, he would finish high school with the rest of his classmates. His parents agreed that as long as he stayed in school, Rashad could live with his mother. To Rashad, it seemed too good to be true. Not only would his sisters be taken care of, he wouldn't have to listen to their fighting and arguing every day. There was even a chance that they might start to cope better with their parents' divorce if they had more attention from family members.

While Rashad had mixed feelings about his mother's remarriage, there was something very exciting about it, too. Rashad would be gaining Gordon as a stepbrother.

Rashad's family has a good chance of blending with Simon and Gordon. Simon has shown respect and courtesy for Rashad and his sisters. Rashad's parents have both remained as involved as possible in making important decisions for the children. With this level of communication between family members, Simon will not seem like a replacement father. In addition, Gordon and Rashad's friendship will promote open communication after their parents are married.

Money

"He spent *our* money on *his* children and *their* mother, and he didn't ask my opinion."

"My stepfather pays for a private school for his own children but I have to go to public school."

"My new wife wants to start a family, but how can I? I already pay half of my salary to my previous family for alimony and child support. As it is there isn't enough money to make ends meet, so how could I support another child?"

A stepfather is the family member most often caught on all sides of the money problem. Since children usually live with their mothers after a divorce, fathers often pay child support to their former wives. A remarried father usually has his wife's children living with him as stepchildren, which adds to household expenses.

Equal opportunity for all children is rarely achieved in any family, nuclear or not. Yet when blended families are involved, the idea of fairness is more elusive as the number of people involved increases.

For instance, the money a man spends to send his biological children to private schools or to buy them a car may jeopardize his relationship with his stepchildren when it is viewed as unfair or favoritism.

Alley's Story

My parents met at a party two years before I was born. At the time, both were recently divorced. My mother had never had any children, but my father had two sons.

It must have been love at first sight, since my parents had a hard time from the start. Hank and Wally, my two halfbrothers, were unwilling to accept that my father would ever love anyone other than their mother. They took every chance possible to make my father feel guilty. If my parents tried to take the boys out to dinner, they refused to go. If my mother invited them to dinner at her house, Hank and Wally were rude during the meal.

I think my mother and father tried really hard to make the boys understand that they were in love. The four of them went to a family counselor for over a year before my parents set a date to get married. My mother says that the counselor helped her and my father to understand what their problems with the boys were, but there weren't any fast solutions.

Two years after my parents married, I was born. Hank and Wally have never been very close to me because they are older than me and only visit once a month. They feel like relatives, they know my family history and love my father, but we don't have much else in common. And then, of course, there is their bad attitude towards my parents' marriage.

Despite the counseling before their marriage, I think that my halfbrothers have continued to make my father feel guilty for his divorce from their mother. They ask for expensive toys and clothes, and they even go to a private school. Hank is the oldest; he just turned fourteen. But he is already talking about the car that my father will buy him when he turns sixteen!

I don't know why my father feels that he has to give the boys everything that they want. Perhaps I'll never understand. But our family will always be under strain as long as Hank and Wally can make my father feel guilty.

While conflicts over money may provoke issues of fairness between biological children and stepchildren, the financial link between former spouses also creates power conflicts.

"Even though I threw my former husband out, he still calls the shots in our lives," explained a single mother. "If he's late with the check, then I can't pay the rent."

This mother views her former spouse's child support payments as continued power over her life. But it is likely that the former husband's new wife has a different view.

"His ex sends the kids over in hand-me-downs so that we will feel guilty," the new stepmother complained, "but it won't work with me. I'm not spending my weekend and *my* money buying clothes for her kids. She already gets half of all of *our* money."

This stepfather is caught in the crossfire. His former wife is unhappy with the arrangement. And the more he tries to appease her, the more his loyalty will appear to be divided to his current wife.

Ky's Story

My parents got divorced when I was a preschooler, and I've lived with my mother ever since. Right after the divorce I spent a lot of time at my grandparents' house while my mother worked. But after I started going to school all day I began living with my mother on a full-time basis.

I used to see my dad on weekends, but when I was about ten he moved to the West Coast. Now I only see him during Christmas for a week and for a month during the summer.

My dad and his new wife have two daughters, ages seven and eight. I always have fun when I visit Dad and his new family. My stepmother is nice to me and she never makes me help with the housework like I do at my mom's house. Although I wouldn't tell my mom, I often daydream that I live with my father year round.

It's hard to see my stepsisters live so differently than I do. After all, I am Dad's kid, too. I'm entitled to live as well as they do! My stepsisters have every toy ever invented. They have beautiful clothes and a stay-home mom who isn't too tired to do things with them after school.

I don't think the girls know how lucky they are. I don't think Dad realizes how unfair it is for me to only live that good life for one month and one week a year.

I know Mom would be terribly hurt if I ever told her I wanted to spend more time at Dad's house. I don't even know if he would want me there. But I'm always depressed for weeks after I come home and fall back into our dull, routine, predictable life. Life is so unfair! Why couldn't Dad provide for us the way he does for my stepsisters?

Dad promised me that he would pay for my college if I keep my grades up for my final two years of high school. I'm hoping that maybe I'll be accepted at a college near Dad so I can get to know him better without hurting Mom's feelings. If that doesn't work out, it's going to be the second biggest disappointment of my life.

The greatest disappointment is that I've had to grow up without Dad being a regular member of our household.

It's clear that the role of the stepmother or stepfather isn't an easy one. Each stepparent has difficulty making a smooth transition into a new family. Whether the problem concerns the discipline of the children or the money spent on them, it is often complicated to find a proper balance between the way stepparents treat their own children and how they treat their stepchildren.

It can be almost impossible to treat children equally all the time, but stepparents who are aware of this problem are more likely to be sensitive to the issue. They may try and prevent unequal treatment. When stepparents are clearly making an effort, all the children in the blended family will, one hopes, respond in a positive and understanding way. Teens appreciate it when their stepparents don't try and discipline them immediately after the family is blended. It's important that emotional bonds are established first. It's important for a teen to express these thoughts to the stepparent. Talking openly and honestly is a great way to solve problems. Then it becomes possible for a stepparent to try and guide a stepchild and help them make important decisions in their lives.

Most importantly, though, stepmothers and stepfathers who do not expect to replace biological mothers and fathers find the transition into a blended family smoother.

CHAPTER 6

Stepsiblings in a Blended Family

Brothers and sisters play together, fight together, and live together. Sometimes they are friends; sometimes they are rivals. Many biological siblings cannot remember a time when their sisters or brothers were not part of the family. They do not compare the before and after period that stepsiblings often experience when families blend.

Remarriage may bring new children into a family. These stepbrothers and stepsisters, or stepsibs for short, may become permanent members of the household, or they may only visit on weekends. Remarried parents sometimes give birth to new children who become halfsiblings to the children already in the blended family.

Parents in nearly all families expect children to get along with one another. Young people in blended families are often given a harder task than just getting along with a sibling. Stepsibs are often expected from the beginning to be "one, big, happy family" with people whom they hardly know.

ARE WE RELATED?

Stepsibs rarely feel close to one another in the beginning. Often the only thing they have in common is that their parents are married to each other. Many times young members of blended families feel overwhelmed in the wake of their parents' decision to start a new family.

While their parents are enjoying a new relationship, the children in blended families are reestablishing themselves. From sharing rooms to sharing pets, adjusting to new stepsibs usually takes six to twenty-four months.

Stepsibs are not legally related to each other. They are kin by virtue of their parents' relationship and marriage. Is it worth the effort to become close to a stepsib if you aren't even related? Yes.

While no one can be forced to create a "big, happy family," stepsibs sometimes become as close as biological siblings. When a remarried parent seems happy and satisfied in the new family, the children will have more incentive to build good relationships with their stepsibs. The parents' happiness and their commitment to the blended family indicate that they are going to be together for a long time, and the children should try and make the best of it.

Successful blended families do not need to strive to mold identical members. Nor do stepsibs need to hold the same values or ideas. As with stepparents, stepsibs should not try to replace biological siblings.

In the beginning, stepsibs and their families should examine and adjust their own expectations in order to appreciate other members' needs and expectations.

Taking time to understand one another and to establish open communication will allow stepsibs to bond more quickly.

EMOTIONS BETWEEN STEPSIBLINGS

Stepchildren come together with different tastes and habits. They also may come with fears, jealousies, and anger. A young person who has been an only child may be excited to have siblings, while a small child may resent any competition for his or her parent's affections.

A year or more may be necessary before stepsibs learn to tolerate their differences. During that time, feelings about each other may range from curiosity to friendship to total hatred.

Will's Story

I'm glad to have a stepfather. My own father died when I was very young, and I barely remember him. My stepfather's name is Bill, which is kind of close to my nickname, Will. At first I called him Bill. I liked that—it sounded like I might have been named after him. After I became more comfortable with Bill, I asked to call him Dad since I do feel that he is my father.

During the school year, there are just the three of us and things run pretty smoothly. But for two months every summer, *they* live with us. My *stepsisters*.

This year will be their third summer with us and probably their last. Laura is seventeen, and Addie is almost nineteen. Addie says that after Laura graduates from high school they don't have to come here anymore. That is the way our dad's custody agreement was written.

Even if you didn't hear my sisters, you would know they were around. Just follow the trail of damp towels, dirty dishes, and hairbrushes. If you still can't find them, check the bathroom. One of them is certain to be in there!

I admit that I don't know my stepsisters very well. We don't fight or argue, but we don't spend much time together either. They seem to have the power over my parents. Whenever Mom or Dad tries to tell them what to do, they say "Our mother never makes us do that." And just like that, they don't have to do it. I can tell that this really upsets Dad, but I'm afraid to ask him about it.

Will didn't have much time during the two months each year to get to know his stepsibs. They were more interested in developing their own lives as young adults and had little interest in getting to know their stepbrother. Addie and Laura also had an unsettled issue with their father and stepmother about their place within the blended family.

With time against them, stepfamilies often remain politely neutral, not wanting to tackle hard issues. Stepsibs in these situations usually are unable to develop many lasting bonds.

COMPETITION AND FAVORITISM

A younger sibling may try to imitate his older brother. Brothers may accuse their parents of preferring a sister over them. Sisters may accuse their parents of preferring a brother over them. Some competition between siblings is natural in any family and helps young people develop a sense of identity.

When a family is blended, stepsiblings may question their places within the family structure. What is their value to the new family?

Will a kindergartner worry that she or he is no longer important now that there is a younger stepsib in the family? If one stepsister has many dates and the other has none, will the dateless sister feel she is too unpopular to be of value?

When stepsibs arrive in their new home it may be difficult to sort out how much rivalry is normal. As remarried parents enjoy their new marriage, young family members need to be reassured that they are still important to their biological parent.

But when parents are busy merging two households, it is easy to understand how stepsibs become jealous and compete for attention. Daily confusion and adjustment may make children feel left out. Stepsibs then desperately crave parental affection.

Stepsibs who are close in age or have similar interests may also feel competitive in the beginning. One of the stepsibs may appear more popular at school, or be a better athlete.

Rivalry often develops in nuclear families, but since stepsibs are not related, the competition may be more intense. If there must be a loser in a stepsibling relationship, what will they lose? A place of value among the stepsibs? The love or respect of a parent?

Stepparents also may treat stepchildren with more tolerance and less discipline. Adults want to welcome stepchildren into their homes and promote good feelings. To natural children, this may seem like the stepsib is replacing their position with their parent.

Competition and favoritism does occur and may get out of hand. But usually they are symptoms of newly blended families struggling for their balance, not a permanent feature of family life. Stepsibs should be encouraged to voice their concerns. As each member of the family finds his or her position in the family, competition will settle down.

Judith's Story

Judith, age eleven, had always been the apple of her parents' eyes. She had four older brothers who were either away at college or living on their own. Judith had been raised almost as an only child for as long as she could remember.

Then Judith's mother fell in love with a colleague who was being transferred to work in Sweden. So Judith's mother and father divorced. The decision was very sudden. No fighting. No crying. No time to adjust.

One evening her parents just told Judith that they were going their separate ways. Because Judith's father did not want her to leave the country, he asked Judith if she would feel comfortable living with him instead of her mother. Judith was too overwhelmed even to think, but she agreed immediately.

Eventually Judith and her father moved into a smaller apartment in the same neighborhood so she didn't have to make new friends or go to a new school. Judith's mother called her every week and wrote often, so although Judith missed her mother terribly, she felt reassured that her mother still loved her.

Judith was mature for her age. She understood that her parents' divorce was because of their differences and that she was not responsible in any way. She also realized that both of her parents still loved her.

After about a year, Judith's father began dating. Judith didn't mind because she knew how lonely her father had been since the divorce. He never discussed his dates with Judith, and she never met his friends. Judith usually asked her friend Sally over to spend the night when her father went out for the evening.

When Judith's father finally found a woman whom he wanted to marry, he asked Judith to have dinner with them. He told Judith how kind and understanding Eileen was, and he explained that he hoped Judith would like her. Judith honestly liked Eileen from the moment they met.

Although Judith knew that Eileen had a daughter one year older than she, Judith never anticipated the rivalry her stepsister, Myra, would cause after her father's remarriage.

Just before the wedding, Judith and her dad moved into Eileen's large home. Judith got a room of her own, next to Myra's beautifully furnished bedroom. At first Judith didn't really mind that Myra had many, many beautiful clothes and possessions. But after several months, when Myra continued to buy extravagant things and Judith's father paid the bills, Judith resented the unequal treatment that neither her stepmother nor her dad seemed to notice.

One night after dinner, Myra modeled a gorgeous dress that she bought to go to a school party. She came downstairs and flitted around, begging for compliments.

"You look great," Judith's dad commented, glancing up from his newspaper. "That shade of green is very becoming on you."

Judith, who sat near her father doing her homework, cringed. She didn't want to share her father's affection with Myra. She resented both her father and Eileen for being so insensitive to her needs. She'd tried to help her father by not creating trouble in their new blended family, but her hostility towards Myra was making Judith miserable.

"Myra is really a pain, Dad," Judith said after her stepsib left the room. "Eileen favors Myra in everything. She fixes Myra's favorite foods and they always go out shopping together. Myra expects to be treated like royalty, and she can be such a snob!"

Judith's father was silent for several long moments; then he said, "I'm glad you trusted me enough to speak up. I didn't mean to just plunge you into our new family and let you fend for yourself. But I guess I've been too busy adjusting myself to see that you've been coping with a lot."

"I can't believe that I was so naive that I thought having a stepsister would be fun! Myra doesn't even speak to me at school; she totally ignores me."

"Cut Myra a little slack," Judith's father suggested. "Myra will never mean as much to me as you do, but I try to be nice to her and let her know that I accept her as a member of our family. I'll speak to Eileen and see if there isn't something we can do to smooth things out a bit. But for now, what do you think about going shopping with me for some new clothes on Saturday?"

"I'd love it!" Judith responded, then asked, "Just the two of us?"

"Just the two of us! I'd enjoy more time together."

Judith was wise to confide in her father when she found it difficult to cope with the favoritism of her stepsib and her stepsib's lack of regard for her. Although Judith was eager to accept Myra as a new member of her family, Myra needed more time to make the transition. When Judith worried that Myra was taking her place in her father's affections, Judith finally reached a crisis level. When Judith shared her feelings with her father, he reassured Judith and alerted his new wife to a potential problem. It is to be hoped that, together, they can prevent it from getting worse.

THE ARRIVAL OF A HALFSIBLING

The arrival of a new baby is an exciting time for a family. People's roles change as they become parents, brothers, sisters, or grandparents. The baby provides a link for the stepfamily. For the first time, the members of the blended family will be related by blood and history. Whether this new link will strengthen or weaken the stepfamily's emotional bond depends partly on the reasons for having the baby and how the family adjusts to the new member.

Remarried couples who are happy and confident in their marriage often want to celebrate their love by raising a child together. When parents make this commitment, the new family member will encourage siblings to build better relationships. Everyone will have confidence that the family is strong. The halfsibling's arrival is an incentive to make the blended family members strive to get along.

Some couples feel they must have a child together to prove that their remarriage is a success. Others believe that a baby will make them a "real" family, in which everyone is related. When a baby is planned for reasons other than love or commitment to the marriage, sibling bonds will be more difficult to form.

A blended family can be close and loving without the addition of a new child. Many families are content with the size of their blended family. Some parents may not have the time or energy to rear more children.

"When I met Larry, I had just been promoted to vice president at the bank. I was happy with my children and wanted to pursue my career. We decided before getting married that my two children were enough. I am comfortable with my remarriage the way it is now."

Young parents who remarry are more likely to have children together. When one partner is young and does not have children, particularly the wife, then the chance that the remarriage will produce a child is greater.

SIBLING RELATIONS WITH HALFSIBLINGS

New siblings may spark old feelings of desertion and anger in children from the parents' former marriages. The attention a halfsibling receives often reminds visiting stepsibs of how little time their natural parent has to share with them. This especially seems true if the new halfsibling arrives before the blended family members have adjusted to their new lifestyle.

Alegra's Story

Alegra became withdrawn after the birth of her half-sister. If her father wanted another baby, she thought, he should have stayed married to her mother. That way, Alegra would have a family where she felt she belonged. Instead her father married Monica, who was much younger than he was. He spent more time with his new wife than anyone else. Alegra was embarrassed to be seen in public with her father and his new wife. Monica looked more like Alegra's older sister than her stepmother.

How long would she have to fight for her father's attention? First she had to compete with Monica, now with her stepmother's crying infant!

Monica even expected Alegra to baby-sit with that noisy child while she went out for the evening with Alegra's father! But Alegra always refused to care for her halfsib, claiming she had too much homework. She had no intentions of ever helping her father's new marriage work smoothly.

Alegra had not coped successfully with her father's remarriage, and she was unable to accept a relationship with her halfsib. She needed to air her hostile feelings with her father, her mother, or a neutral party such as a family counselor to develop some insight on how to handle her anger.

STEPSIBS AS ADULTS

After years of living together, sharing experiences and relatives, stepsibs still have a voluntary relationship with each other. Blended families often are not fully recognized as true families by the stepsibs. As a result, when young people move away from their parents and start independent lives of their own, many often feel less obligated to keep in contact with their stepsibs and half-sibs than with their biological siblings.

A good indicator of how strong step- and halfsibling relationships are is how the siblings fare in adulthood. Researchers have studied adults with half- and stepsibs and found that, in general, children of remarriages do consider their step- and halfsiblings to be "real" family. But these children still give greater priority to full biological siblings.

When couples remarry in their later years, after all their children are adults and living in separate households, the bonds between the stepsibs are often insignificant. This is particularly true if the adult children live in distant locations and rarely see one another.

Adult children of newly blended families who live in close proximity may or may not interact or bond with each other. Much depends on the needs and personalities of the new stepparent and his or her children.

DO STEP- AND HALFSIBLINGS MATTER?

Social scientists are curious about the link between step- and halfsiblings. As the divorce rate climbs, children have fewer full siblings and more step- and halfsiblings. Children growing up in blended families often maintain contact with their step- and halfsiblings as adults, but what about the quality of these relationships?

Can you imagine phoning your stepsister right after the birth of your first child? Would you be willing to help your stepbrother care for your elderly stepparent?

Siblings, whether step or not, will have closer ties in adulthood if they are closer in age and live near each other as adults. Another factor in how close you feel to your stepsiblings is the length of time they have spent in the blended family.

The longer a blended family lives together, the more likely those relationships will last long after the stepsibs move out of the house. While this seems obvious, keep in mind that nearly 60 percent of all remarriages end in divorce. This does not leave much time for children to develop close ties with their step- and halfsiblings.

Children in a blended family *do* matter to each other. They may never develop a close relationship, but through continued, daily contact they will affect each other and their family's dynamics. In the future, the large number of adults with half- and stepsiblings will change how we all view the idea of the family.

CHAPTER 7

Helping Yourself, Helping Your Family

You've seen that establishing a new family takes a lot of time and effort from all of the family members—including you. If you don't participate in helping your blended family overcome obstacles and create new bonds, you are making life more difficult for yourself and your family. By taking an active role in your new blended family, you will ease the transition for yourself, and your family will appreciate your enthusiasm and cooperation. You will also feel better about your situation because you have taken some control over it. You will also benefit by improving your ability to communicate and negotiate. These are valuable skills to have in all aspects of your life. Being a member of a blended family gives you a chance to learn new skills, share in new experiences and family traditions. You may even get to experience a new culture if your parent marries or becomes involved with someone of a different race or nationality. As part of the blended family, you learn about and come to respect traditions and ways that seemed very different at first. But by respecting your new family members and their traditions, you will discover the art of compromise and begin to get along. The strength of your blended family will come from listening and learning from one another.

COMMUNICATION

It doesn't help any problem to pretend it doesn't exist. Confronting matters head-on is the best way to deal with them. How can you be part of the solution? The Stepfamily Association of Illinois suggests sitting down with your family and going over a list of common myths among blended families. By comparing some of your expectations with the realities that exist in your family, it will help you all understand each other a little better. The following is a list of common myths that are problematic for blended families. Gather together with your family and read each one aloud. Then discuss how everyone feels about it. Is it a realistic expectation to have? How does your family differ from these common, yet often unrealistic expectations? Give everyone equal time to speak and try to be sure that everyone remains open to different opinions. Keep in mind that you might not agree all the time.

- A blended family forms only after the death of a parent, and the surviving parent decides to remarry.
- If the children are all grown, a remarriage does not form a blended family.
- Remarrying biological parents who have grown, independent children do not have to deal with most of the problems that blended families with younger children do.

- The parents and children in a normal blended family live in one home.
- Blended families are pretty much the same as traditional families.
- The rules that applied to your old family will work well with this new family.
- If we encounter any major problems in our family, we can expect love and support from our friends and relatives.
- The problems that existed in our old families and/or households will not affect the success of our new family. The past is the past.
- Even though my parent and I have lived as a single-parent family for a while, we can incorporate new family members into our household with ease.
- Everyone will be treated equally in our new family.
- When I have a conflict with a stepsibling or stepparent, my biological parent should always side with me.
- In a healthy blended family, everyone loves each other. If they don't, they are bad or wrong.
- The remarriage (or cohabitation) automatically gives each stepparent the authority to discipline the other's children.
- An effective stepparent should share in the child-discipline responsibilities right away.
- There will be no favoritism in our blended family.
- All our relatives from both sides should treat all the children and stepchildren equally at holidays and special family occasions.
- Whether my stepparent chooses to adopt me or not, he or she still has the same legal rights and obligations as my biological parent.

- None of the children in our blended family will ever change residence to live with their other biological parent.
- This remarriage or cohabitation should not cause any members of the blended family to experience any losses.
- The grieving process should be over by now, so our blended family does not have to worry about other family members mourning the deceased parent.
- It's unnecessary for divorced parents to explain clearly why they divorced to their biological children.
- Stepchildren often don't succeed as well.
- It's solely the parent's responsibility for making everyone happy.
- Being a stepparent is the same as being a biological parent.
- Stepparents are not as good as biological parents.
- Stepfamilies are not as good as traditional families.
- There's no chance that anyone in our blended family will ever be romantically attracted to, or sexually active, with each other, except the married adults.
- No one will resent it if each parent spends time alone with their biological children.
- It's okay to require stepkids to call a stepparent "Mom" or "Dad", even if they don't want to.
- Blended family members have no special reasons to ever feel guilty or embarrassed.
- The children's other biological parents are not, and never will be, full members of our blended family.
- The money that is provided from ex-spouses will be used fairly in our family.

- The children's other biological parents will never remarry or have new children.
- The children's other parents will never sue for child custody.
- The stepchildren would be happy and excited if the stepparent wishes to legally adopt them.
- Having another child will surely strengthen our blended family.
- Most communities have effective support groups and provide informed education for blended families and their problems.
- This blended family will never end in another divorce.

Those are a lot of myths to discuss. It may be beneficial to pick out the ones that are the most relevant to your family and concentrate on them. Once you've had a chance to talk about them with your family, you will most likely discover how different everyone's expectations are and how different those expectations can be from the realities that exist. Facing the realities can be very difficult. Blended families may look to support groups, clergy members, relatives, and community based programs for help. Sometimes, however, blended families need to seek psychiatric counseling for some family members who are having a particularly stressful time. It's up to the family to decide what type of help is best for all of the members. However, some experts suggest considering additional counseling if a family member feels:

- alone handling the losses;
- torn between two households or parents;
- excluded from the family;

- isolated by overwhelming feelings of guilt or anger;
- uncomfortable with any member of the blended family.

Also, experts strongly recommend getting psychiatric counseling if:

- a child unleashes his or her anger out on a particular family member;
- this anger causes one of the parents a great amount of stress and he or she is therefore unable to handle the child's behavior;
- a stepparent or biological parent openly favors one of the children, or a child openly resents a stepparent or a biological parent;
- the disciplinary role falls solely into the hands of the biological parent;
- a family member has great difficulty enjoying any normal activities that involve the blended family as a whole or has great difficulty functioning at school or work.

STEPFAMILY FOUNDATION

The Stepfamily Foundation was formed in 1975 to cater to the needs of the growing number of blended families in the United States. The founder and president is Jeannette Lofas, CSW, and she is recognized as the definitive expert on step relationships. In 1995, Ms. Lofas was awarded the National Parents' Day Award by President Clinton, which acknowledged her organization in its efforts to help strengthen blended families across the country.

The foundation offers counseling sessions and may be helpful to your family. It devises a specific plan of action for each family that includes:

- defining job descriptions, i.e. rules and responsibilities for each family member;
- the allocation of time, energy, and money spent on the blended family;
- building strength by increasing communication and developing negotiating skills for all family members;
- handling ex-spouses, discipline, manners, and visitation rights.

It is the foundation's goal that the counseling be short term and positive. Most blended families respond very well and report benefits after the first session. Most of the counseling for blended families lasts between eight and ten sessions, during which families receive many materials, such as books and videos, to aid in their therapy. Sessions can be expensive. If your family cannot afford professional counseling, there are other options available. For example, the Stepfamily Foundation has a crisis hot line that gives free counseling for the first thirty minutes. There may be other organizations in your community that offer similar services. Another option is to join the foundation. A membership will cost $70, but the contribution is tax deductible. Included with the membership is the following:

Books
Living in Step, by Jeannette Lofas and Ruth Roosevelt.
Stepparenting, by Jeannette Lofas.

Videotapes
Family Matters: The Realities of Step. 30 minutes.

Audiotapes
How to be a Stepparent. 60 minutes.

Newsletters
One year's subscription to New American Family, the
Stepfamily Foundation's official newsletter.
Sample issues of the New American Family Newsletter.

Booklets
Stepfamily Foundation brochure.
Resources:
    Ten Steps Digest
    Dynamics of Step
    Stepfamily Statistics

There is also a limited basic information packet available for only a $25 tax-deductible contribution. Look in
the help list at the back of this book to contact the Stepfamily Foundation. These materials may help your family
adjust to the transition on its own. Again, these types of
decisions should be discussed among all family members.
The decision to participate in therapy should include the
whole family. Being aware of the resources available is the
first step towards helping you and your family. There are
other organizations that offer similar programs and counseling. The Stepfamily Association of Illinois offers help
on their Web site, which you'll also find in the help list at
the back of this book.

With the proper awareness and education, you and your
family can meet and successfully handle the challenges of
a blended family. As the numbers of blended families

continue to grow, the number of help organizations and resources will grow. In the year 2000 blended families will outnumber traditional, nuclear families in the United States. Hopefully, this will bring about more understanding and more options as our definition of what a family means expands and grows to include all the different types of families that exist.

Glossary

alimony   Money paid to a former spouse for the purchase of basic necessities such as food, clothing, and shelter.

biological relative   A person related through blood.

blended family   Family whose members are linked by combinations of marriage, divorce, death, and remarriage. Blended families always include children.

bonding   Special emotional tie to another person.

child support   Money ordered by the court to be paid to the custodial parent by the other parent to maintain a child's well-being after his or her parents' divorce.

cope   To learn to understand and adjust to one's problems.

counselor   Person trained to listen to children and adults and to help them understand their feelings, worries, and confusion.

custodial parent   The parent who has the legal responsibility for raising the child or children after a divorce.

custody   Possession, control, and assumption of legal responsibility of a minor child by a parent.

divorce   The legally declared end of a marriage between husband and wife.

expectations   Hopes for a specific outcome.

foster care   When the state legally assumes custody of minors to protect them from abuse or neglect and places them in the care of qualified, paid adults.

joint custody   Possession, control, and assumption of legal responsibility for a minor child by two nonmarried adults.

minor   Person below the age of eighteen or twenty-one. Each state defines the age at which a person is no longer considered a minor.

mourning   The act of expressing sadness due to a loss.

noncustodial parent   Parent who no longer has legal responsibility for a child's welfare after the parents have divorced or separated. The noncustodial parent may have visitation rights.

nuclear family   Husband, wife, and all the children belonging to that marriage.

visitation   Scheduled time during which a child and his or her noncustodial parent will visit. It is usually a specific schedule of weekends, school vacations, or other days.

Where to Go for Help

ADDRESSES, INFORMATION, AND RESOURCES

Loss of a Parent

Mothers Against Drunk Drivers (MADD)
5330 Primrose, Suite 146
Fair Oaks, CA 95628

The Compassionate Friends
P.O. Box 3696
Oak Brook, IL 69522

The Dougy Center
3909 SE 52nd Avenue
P.O. Box 86852
Portland, OR 97268
(503) 775-5683
The Dougy Center provides information for teens who have lost a loved one. Contact them for support groups in your area.

Single Parents

New Beginnings, Inc.
612 Kennebec Avenue
Takoma Park, MD 20912
(301) 587-9233
This national organization provides support groups, skills exchanges, and family activities for the newly single parent.

94

Parents Without Partners
410 North Michigan Avenue
Chicago, IL 60611
(312) 644-6610 or (800) 638-8078
Local chapters exist across the country. International Youth Council provides support and social events for teens between the ages of twelve and seventeen who live in single-parent families. To find a local chapter, call the toll-free number or check your telephone directory.

Grandparents as Parents

GAP: Grandparents as Parents
Psychiatric Clinic for Youth
2801 Atlantic Avenue
Long Beach, CA 90801
(213) 595-3151

Second Time Around Parents
Family and Community Service of Delaware County
100 West Front Street
Medina, PA 19063
(215) 566-7540

Forming a Blended Family

American Association for Marriage and Family Therapy
1133 15th Street NW, Suite 300
Washington, DC 20005-2710
(202) 452-0109
e-mail: webmgr@aamft.org

Joint Custody Association
10606 Wilkins Avenue
Los Angeles, CA 90024
(213) 475-5352

Rainbows
1111 Tower Road
Schaumberg, IL 60173
(847) 310-1880
Web site: http://rainbows.org
Provides materials, leader training, and consultation for organizations sponsoring divorces, death, and remarriage.

Stepfamily Association of America, Inc.
215 Centennial Mall South, Suite 212
Lincoln, NE 68508
(402) 477-STEP or (800) 735-0329

Stepfamily Association of Illinois
P.O. Box 3124
Oak Park, IL 60303
(708) 848-0909
Web site: http://www.parentsplace.com

Stepfamily Foundation
33 West End Avenue
New York, NY 10023
Telephone: (212) 877-3244 or (800) SKY-STEP
24-hour information line: (212) 799-STEP
Crisis line/Hot line: (212) 744-6924
Web site: http://www.stepfamily.org

Hot Lines

Childhelp: (800) 422-4453
Parents Anonymous: (800) 421-0353

Newsletters

Stepfamilies
A sixteen page quarterly from the Stepfamily Association of America.
For information call (800) 735-0329

Step Up
Americas first independent newsletter for stepfamilies. It's four to six pages, including information for teens.
For information call (219) 938-6962

Life's Landmines to Landscapes
A ten-page independent newsletter for stepfamily information, education, and encouragement.
For information call (504) 443-1449

Board Games

LifeStories
A win-win boardgame that provides entertaining conversation between family, friends, and people who have just met. Ages 6 to 106.
For information: FNDI Partnership, 701 Decater Avenue, #104, Golden Valley, MN 55427

FutureStories
A similar game for family and friends to share hopes and dreams.
For information: FNDI Partnership (see address above)

The Ungame
A noncompetitive game to help adults and teens learn safely about each other.

For information: FSA Publications, 11700 W. Lake Park Drive, Milwaukee, WI, 53224, (414) 359-1040

Divorce Cope
A board game, for ages eight and up, to help adults and teens talk about events and feelings related to divorce and remarriage.
For information: Theraplay, Inc., P.O. Box 762, Monsey, NY, 10952, (212) 991-1909

In Canada

Canadian Stepfamily Association
P.O. Box 96, SII, R.R. #4
Colborne, ON K0K 1S0
Web site: http://www.eagle.ca/~jcollar
e-mail: stepfamily@eagle.ca

For Further Reading

Bailey, Marilyn. *Stepfamilies*. New York: Crestwood House, 1990.

Berman, Claire. *What Am I Doing in a Stepfamily?* New York: Lyle Stuart, 1992.

Bernstein, Sharon C. *A Family That Fights*. Morton Grove, IL: Albert Whitman & Company, 1991.

Bode, Janet. *Death Is Hard to Live With*. New York: Delacorte Press, 1993.

Getzoff, Ann, and Carolyn McClenahan. *Stepkids: A Survival Guide for Teenagers in Stepfamilies*. New York: Walker, 1984.

Kaplan, Leslie S. *Coping with Stepfamilies*, rev. ed. New York: Rosen Publishing Group, 1991.

Krementz, Jill. *How It Feels When Parents Divorce*. New York: Alfred A. Knopf, Inc., 1984.

Rosenberg, Maxine B. *Living With A Single Parent*. New York: Bradbury Press, 1992.

Walters, Laura Sherman. *There's a New Family in My House!* Wheaton, IL: Harold Shaw Publishers, 1993.

Index

JOHN STEINBECK LIBRARY

JAN 2001
RECEIVED
Salinas Public
Library